Betwe[en] the Lines

by David Hill

Contents

CW01638932

CAMBRIDGE
UNIVERSITY PRESS

Chapter 1

Jerome and Caleb and I play in a band. In fact, we're the whole band.

We call ourselves LINE3 because there are just three of us – until last week, anyway – and because we write all the lines of our songs.

We write the songs together in Caleb's basement. I usually think up a first line. Then Caleb and Jerome start adding other ones. I think up some more lines, and it goes on like that. We work off one another, and it feels cool. When we've got the lines, we start building the music around them.

Just after we got together to start LINE3, we worked up a song that started with a line of mine,

Life sux; the world is black.

When he heard it, Jerome went, "Cool, Brad." Then he said,

Time for me to cut some slack.

Caleb came in with,

I'm on my way; I won't be back,
You'll find me on some far-off track.

We kicked it around, added bits and cut out bits, and it ended up as LINE3's first song. We sang it at the high school Talent Quest Show and came second.

Chapter 2

Then last week two things happened. First, LINE3 got invited to play at a school dance. We were excited. It was going to be our biggest show yet.

Second, we got a fourth person in the band. A girl named Saskia, who sings. She's Caleb's cousin's cousin, and she's got this brilliant clear voice.

But it wasn't her voice I noticed the first time I met Saskia. It was... well, her. She's nice-looking, with this amazing long hair. Plus she's shy, but really friendly. I knew straightaway that I wanted to write some lines for her. Lines that would make her really notice me.

I didn't tell Caleb and Jerome, of course. I knew what they'd say. But I spent Friday night and most of Saturday thinking up all sorts of cool lines for our practice on Sunday.

Chapter 3

I got to Caleb's place just after two o'clock. He and Jerome were already down in the basement. The three of us were going to work on some lines before Saskia came at three.

"We have to get some really great stuff," Jerome said. "This school dance is our big chance, guys."

"Right," said Caleb. "You got some ideas, Brad?"

I didn't want them to guess how I felt about Saskia, so I just shrugged and said, "A couple. How about this?"

Your eyes are like the morning sky.

They both looked blank for a moment. Then Jerome grinned and said,

They're turning red while I walk by.

Caleb grinned, too, and said,

And one's been hit by a seagull pie.

They both started laughing and chucking cushions at each other. "Nah, that's pretty sad, Brad," Caleb told me.

"All right," I said, though I didn't feel all right. I felt a bit annoyed. "Try this one,"

Your face reminds me of a rose.

They looked blank again. Then they both spoke at once,

It wobbles when the cold wind blows,
There's prickles growing up its nose.

The next minute they were laughing and falling about again. I didn't laugh. I was starting to get pissed off.

"Nah," said Jerome. "That's really bad, Brad."

Chapter 4

They calmed down after a minute. "Come on," Jerome told us. "We've got to get something really brilliant for the dance at school. We need some lines before Saskia comes. Any other ideas, Brad?"

I didn't say anything at first. I didn't want to come up with more lines if they were going to keep laughing at me. But after a while I said, "Here's one, maybe."

You're really something when you dance.

This time they both started laughing together. They both spoke together,

You're like a zombie in a trance.
Have you got spiders in your pants?

They pretended to fall down on the floor and die. I just stood and watched them. These guys were supposed to be my friends. If they kept on like this, I was going to whack one of them.

Finally they got up. "Nah," said Caleb. "That's the worst you've had, Brad."

I could feel my fists going tight. We often made jokes and fooled around while we were working on lines, but didn't Jerome and Caleb realise who my lines were about? No, I thought – of course they didn't. And I didn't want them to either.

Jerome must have seen that I was getting angry. "Sorry," he said. "Hey, it'll come. Let's hear another line."

I kept my voice as calm as I could. I looked straight at them, and I said,

I hear your voice. It calls my name.

Caleb made a sort of snorting noise and said,

No, sorry – it's just a blocked drain.

Jerome made a snorting noise, too, and he said,

Never mind – they sound the same.

Next minute, they were laughing and jumping around and punching each other on the arm. Once again, I just stood and watched them. But I could feel my neck getting hotter and hotter. No, I wasn't going to whack one of these guys. I was going to whack both of them, both of my so-called friends.

Chapter 5

At last they stopped laughing and tried to look serious. "We're just feeling a bit mad, Brad," said Jerome. Caleb nodded. "You don't look too glad, Brad." They both started snorting and punching each other again. Any minute now, I was going to join that punching.

Suddenly, Caleb looked at his watch. "Hey, Saskia's going to be here in five minutes. We have to think of something for the dance."

Jerome nodded. "Sorry, Brad. Didn't mean to put you down. Tell us anything else you've got, eh?"

When I spoke, I could hear that my voice sounded tight. "I've got two more lines. If you guys stuff them up, then we're finished, right?"

Now they both looked worried. "We won't, Brad," Jerome told me. Caleb nodded.

"All right," I said. "I'll say them both. You'd better think real hard." I took a slow breath. I thought of Saskia's long hair, and I said,

Your hair is like a mountain stream.

Then I thought of the way she talked, and I went on,

Your voice is quiet, soft and pure.

For a second, my two so-called friends kept looking serious. Then they both started to shake. Caleb said,

Your hair is like a mountain stream.
When it gets warm, it starts to steam.

And Jerome added,

Your voice is quiet, soft and pure.
I need to buy some horse manure.

That's it, I knew. That's the end of LINE3. That's the end of these guys as my friends.

Chapter 6

Then three things happened at once. Caleb and Jerome began to laugh. I started to take a step forward and lift up my fists. And the door opened, and Saskia walked in.

"Hi, guys," she said. "Got some cool lines for me to sing?"

We all stared at her. I saw her long hair and her shy smile. Before I could stop, I heard myself say,

Your eyes are like the morning sky.

Straightaway, Jerome and Caleb began making more snorting noises. But Saskia just looked at me. It was a different look from any that she'd given me before. The look seemed to go right into me.

"That's sweet, Brad," she said. Then her cheeks went pink. "Hey, I'm going to get a drink of water, eh?" she told Caleb and Jerome. "Then we can get started." She left the room.

Caleb and Jerome stood looking at me, too. They were silent for a moment. Then Caleb nodded, and Jerome spoke.

"Yeah. That's...that's not too bad, Brad. That'll be cool for LINE3."

I shook my head. "There isn't any more LINE3," I told them. They stared at me, and then they both began to say something.

"Hey, you don't mean that. We...." said Jerome.

"We were just kidding. You know...." added Caleb.

But I stopped them. "Yeah. From now on, we're LINE4."